What's the Weather? / ¿Qué tiempo hace?

IT'S WINDY!/ ¡ESTÁ VENTOSO!

By Alex Appleby

Traducción al español: Eduardo Alamán

Gareth Stevens Publishing

Please visit our website, www.garethstevens.com. For a free color catalog of all our high-quality books, call toll free 1-800-542-2595 or fax 1-877-542-2596.

Library of Congress Cataloging-in-Publication Data

Appleby, Alex.
It's windy = Esta ventoso / by Alex Appleby.
p. cm. — (What's the weather = ¿Qué tiempo hace?)
Parallel title: Esta ventoso
In English and Spanish.
Includes index.
ISBN 978-1-4339-9452-4 (library binding)
1. Winds — Juvenile literature. I. Appleby, Alex. II. Title.
QC931.4 A66 2014
551.518—dc23

First Edition

Published in 2014 by
Gareth Stevens Publishing
111 East 14th Street, Suite 349
New York, NY 10003

Editor: Ryan Nagelhout
Designer: Andrea Davison-Bartolotta
Spanish Translation: Eduardo Alamán

All illustration by Michael Harmon

Printed in the United States of America

CPSIA compliance information: Batch #CS13GS: For further information contact Gareth Stevens, New York, New York at 1-800-542-2595.

Contents

Contenido

It is windy!

¡Está ventoso!

The wind moves clouds over my head.

El viento mueve las nubes sobre mi cabeza.

The elm tree in my yard is shaking.

El viento sacude el olmo de mi patio.

Wind makes it feel colder outside.

Cuando salimos, el viento nos hace sentir más frío.

I wear a blue jacket
when it's windy.

Cuando está ventoso
uso una chamarra azul.

Winds can be strong! This is called a gust.

¡Los vientos pueden ser fuertes! A esto se le llama ráfagas.

It blows off my blue hat!

¡Las ráfagas se llevan
mi sombrero azul!

I chase after my hat.
It lands in a green bush.

Persigo mi sombrero.
Se detiene en un
arbusto verde.

Other winds are lighter.
This is a breeze.

Otros vientos son leves.
Se les llama brisa.

The wind helps me fly my red kite!

¡El viento hace volar mi cometa roja!

Words to Know/ Palabras que debes saber

bush/
(el) arbusto

clouds/
(las) nubes

elm tree/
(el) olmo

Index / Índice